Bone Broth

*The Ultimate Bone Broth Recipes For
Wellness And Optimal Health*

By Susan T. Williams

This book is designed to provide information on the topic covered. The information herein is offered for informational purposes solely. It is sold with the understanding that neither the author nor the publisher is engaged in rendering legal, accounting or other professional services. If legal or other professional advice is warranted, the services of an appropriate professional should be sought.

While every effort has been made to make the information presented here as complete and accurate as possible, it may contain errors, omissions or information that was accurate as of its publication but subsequently has become outdated by marketplace or industry changes. Neither author nor publisher accepts any liability or responsibility to any person or entity with respect to any loss or damage alleged to have been caused, directly or indirectly, by the information, ideas, opinions or other content in this book.

In no way, is it legal to reproduce, duplicate, or transmit any part of this document in either electronic means or printed form. Recording of this publication is strictly prohibited and any storage of this document is not allowed unless with written permission from the publisher.

The use of any trademark within this book is for clarifying purposes only, and any trademarks referenced in this work are used are without consent, and remain the property of the respective trademark holders, who are not affiliated with the publisher or this book.

© Copyright 2016 by The Total Evolution - All rights reserved.

Table of Contents

Introduction 5

Chapter 1: The Roots of Bone Broth 7

Chapter 2: The Benefits of Bone Broth 11

Chapter 3: Bone Broth and the Paleo Diet 17

Chapter 4: Basic Broths, Stocks and Soups ... 19

Chapter 5: Bone Broth Drinks and Smoothies 53

Chapter 6: Bone Broth Breakfast Recipes 63

Chapter 7: Bone Broth Sauces and Sides 81

Conclusion 89

Preview Of 'Mediterranean Diet: The Complete Mediterranean Diet For Beginners With 101 Heart Healthy Recipes' 91

Our Other Books 96

Introduction

There are many health books that have been written over the years on how you can detox, cleanse and heal your mind, body and spirit. Thousands of studies have been done, and research papers have been written regarding what people should eat to live a consciously healthy life.

One thing you'll notice is that there's always fresh research that comes out and debunks the findings of a previous health study. One minute we are told to eat more of a certain food for the benefit of our health, the next minute research is released showing that we should eat less of it if we want to stay healthy. For someone who is always following current health trends, it can be a wicked roller coaster ride that ends up in frustration. If medical scientists can't seem to agree on anything conclusively, then what should we do?

Fortunately, you do not have to be concerned about divergent scientific research when it comes to *bone broth*. Evidence is mounting by the day regarding the powerful health benefits of bone broth. And what makes it even better is that bone broth has been around forever!

Bone broth can be described as a 'prehistoric' food, with archeologists discovering proof that people long ago used to cook bone broth in the stomachs of animals, way before crockpots and other cookware were invented. Bone broth has been shown to be a gut-cleanser, improving your digestive health and triggering numerous other health benefits like relief of joint pain and even weight loss.

In this book you will learn the history of bone broth, its numerous benefits, and also how it is linked to the Paleo diet. There are also 40 mouth watering recipes that you will absolutely love – soups, smoothies, sides and even breakfast dishes!

After reading this book and trying out the recipes, I'm sure you'll turn into a loyal bone broth fanatic!

Here's to wellness and optimal health!

CHAPTER 1

The Roots of Bone Broth

Bone broth is not a new trend. Making bone broth is actually an ancient tradition that goes as far back as the early Stone Age period. When our human ancestors were discovering fire and how to make simple tools, their main source of nutrition was animals. They may not have made bone broth like we do today, but they seemed to have had an innate knowledge of the nutritional benefits of bone marrow, as suggested by archeological findings.

It is difficult to pin down exactly when our ancestors first started to boil bones in water and simmer them with plants and herbs, but what we do know is that bone broth soon spread to all parts of the world. Every human culture, in one way or another, soon made this savory broth a staple of their diet. Today, bone broth has become a major ingredient used by many chefs to enhance different types of dishes, due to its rich and complex nature.

Bone broth, also referred to as bone stock, is made from the bones of grass-fed animals, pasture-raised poultry or pigs, or fish caught in the wild. The bones are slowly simmered in water for many hours so as to extract essential minerals and amino acids. Bones happen to be the most dense and deepest tissues in the body, so in essence you are cooking the root of the animal.

Most of us can still remember the time when we were growing up when bone broth was the go-to food for healing and restoration though we may not have referred to it as such. If you had a tummy ache, grandma made you some soup. If you came down with the flu or had a cold, a steaming mug of chicken soup was always at hand. In fact, by the 19th Century, bone broth, or "invalid beef tea" as it was known then, was primarily viewed as a beverage for people who were sick. Not only was it part of the home diet, but hospital kitchens made it as well.

As the 20th Century rolled in, farming was still widespread, and many small farmers who kept their own animals saw bone broth as a way of maximizing the use of every last piece of carcass. There were different varieties of bone broth made in households, and it was a staple at every meal.

But with urbanization and modernization, traditional organic bone broth started fading away from most kitchens – until now. In the West, bone broth has come back with a loud bang. However, in the rest of the world, it never went away. In the East, it has always been regarded as a healing beverage that promotes strength, growth of red blood cells and enhances functioning of the liver and kidneys.

For those who have adopted the Paleo diet, drinking bone broth fits right into the Paleo lifestyle. It's important to note that bone broth shouldn't be treated like the superfood du jour or a trend that will be gone tomorrow. It has many nutritious properties that even medical and wellness specialists recognize.

But here's the thing. That store-bought bone broth that comes in a can, box or bouillon cube will not give you the nutrients you need. It may be the easy way to make broth, but it's just full of artificial favors that won't do you any good.

If you truly want to enjoy the numerous and varied healing properties of bone broth, you have to make it the right way. Remember – you cannot substitute organic bone broth made in the traditional way!

CHAPTER 2

The Benefits of Bone Broth

Bone broth is much more than just a beverage. It is food that nourishes our digestive system and helps it soak in as many nutrients as possible without using up too much energy. Bone broth is a low-calorie food that builds and maintains our bodies.

So why do we bother boiling bones in water for so long anyway? Well, this slow and lengthy simmering of bones enables all the nutrients in them to be extracted and deposited into the water. In most cases, some type of acid is added (usually apple cider vinegar) in order to maximize the breakdown and extraction of proteins and minerals. This is similar to what our own stomachs acids do.

So what are some of the health benefits of bone broth that wellness advocates, naturopathic physicians, nutritionists, and alternative healthcare providers have been raving about? Here are some reasons why you should eat bone broth:

- It repairs your bone tissue and joints.
- It improves your nails, skin and hair.
- It alleviates acne.
- It boosts your fertility and sexual function.
- It cures cold and flu.
- It helps in weight loss.
- It maintains the wellness of expectant mothers.
- It strengthens a patient prior to surgery.
- It helps the body heal after surgery.
- It helps heal wounds and injuries.
- It relieves autoimmune diseases such as Crohn's disease and rheumatoid arthritis.

It's plain to see why bone broth is considered good for your overall health. With such a long list of health benefits, it is no wonder that society is now experiencing a bone broth revival.

Breaking Down the Broth

For years, our ancestors consumed bone broth, knowing very well that it was an elixir for healing and wellness. But what is it about this ancient superfood that makes it so special? Let's break it down and see the basic components that make up this nutritional powerhouse.

Cartilage

Bones consist of cartilage, which is full of collagen, elastin, chondroitin sulfate and glucose. The major benefit of cartilage in bone both is that it promotes the health of the skin as well as joints. Skin and joints are two areas that deteriorate due to ageing, so if you want to stay fresh and young, get yourself some bone broth.

The collagen found in cartilage is responsible for controlling numerous cell functions. Collagen usually presents itself in bone broth in the form of gelatin. This protein compound is what gives bone broth its unique therapeutic reputation. It helps your wounds and soft tissues heal faster after an injury or post-surgery, while also helping to form and repair damaged or bruised bone tissue. Collagen also aids in the formation and repair of the mucous membrane that protects the gastrointestinal tract.

Bone Marrow

Marrow is full of dense and nutrient-rich vitamins, essential fatty acids and lipids, and minerals that provide power and energy. Ever wondered why a predator can never wait to sink its teeth into the bones of its prey? They want to suck the marrow out because it offers an instant and strong energy boost!

Bone marrow is believed to boost the immune system, which is why chicken broth is a favorite remedy for colds, coughs and the flu. It also improves clotting of blood, and helps get oxygen to cells. Bone marrow is known to also ease digestion problems, relieve irritable bowel syndrome and help combat diseases like cancer.

Amino Acids

These are the key building blocks of the body's tissues. The most important essential amino acids found in bone broth are:

Glycine – Boosts oxygenation of blood; heals wounds; strengthens the immune system and helps repair other proteins within the body.

Proline – Helps produce collagen; tightens and strengthens cell structures; heals wounds; helps heal leaky gut syndrome and reduces the appearance of cellulite.

Minerals and Vitamins

The microelements found in the bone marrow include calcium, phosphorous, magnesium, sulfur, selenium, zinc and many other minerals. Marrow also contains a heavy concentration of vitamin A. Eating marrow is better than taking expensive supplements, as it contains these microelements in their raw and natural form in the perfect concentration. These minerals are known to repair damaged nerve endings, improve cardiovascular function, and stimulate sexual function. On top of that, they also boost your memory, emotional mood and sleep.

There is no doubt that bone broth is chock-full of healthy nutrients that are naturally designed to restore the body and provide it with everything it needs. Always remember that a healthy gut is a healthy body, so take care of your digestive system and it will take care of you!

CHAPTER 3

Bone Broth and the Paleo Diet

The Paleo diet is based on the types of foods presumed to have been eaten by early humans, consisting chiefly of meat, fish, vegetables, and fruit, and excluding dairy or grain products and processed food. If you are starting out on your journey to embrace the Paleo lifestyle, then you should seriously consider making homemade bone broth a key part of your diet. Bone broth tastes delicious and is also good for you, so integrating it into your diet is any easy way to boost your overall health.

If you intend to cook any dish that incorporates a piece of meat or vegetable, then bone broth would be a great addition. It can also be used in all kinds of soups, stews, sauces and curries.

Most people on the Paleo diet tend to overlook bone broth as a source of nutrition. Apart from your regular consumption of fruits, vegetables, meats and animal fat, bones should play a primary role in your diet. The price of bones is actually much less than that of organ meats, so if you end up making use of all the bones from that chicken or beef ribs you bought, they will cost you nothing. For this reason, you should go for bone-in meats whenever possible. Alternatively, just enquire from your butcher and you will be able to get some bones for a really cheap price.

Another good thing about bone broth is that it can be made from different animal bones, e.g. bones from fish, lamb, pork, beef, turkey, or chicken. If you can get your hands on some wild game meat, then you should know that the healthiest bones come from wild animals because they consume food that is naturally designed for their digestive systems. This means their bones contain all the nutritional goodness you need.

A good Paleo lifestyle should be healthy as well as fun, and bone broth offers you an opportunity to get creative in the kitchen. Bone broth can be used every time you are cooking a dish that requires a liquid, so you are free to go ahead and come up with as many uses of bone broth as you want!

CHAPTER 4

Basic Broths, Stocks and Soups

Roast Chicken Stock

This recipe is full of vital minerals, gelatin, chondroitin and glucosamine. These are minerals and amino acids that specifically heal your gut and help protect you from colds and flu. This meal is easy and inexpensive to make, and incorporates a nutritious and deep flavor. Adding apple cider vinegar enables more minerals to be released from the chicken bones.

Serves: 2

Ingredients:

8 cups (½ gallon) cold water

Vegetable scraps (carrot peels, celery leaves, garlic, onion trimmings)

1 leftover roast chicken carcass

1 tbsp apple cider vinegar

2 bay leaves

Method:

Strip the scraps of meat from the chicken carcass.

Place the carcass, bay leaves and vegetables into a crockpot.

Cover the carcass with filtered water.

Add the vinegar.

Cook the mixture slowly over low heat for over 24 hours.

Sieve the broth using a fine mesh strainer, and pour into mason jars.

Grass-Fed Beef Stock

Beef broth is the perfect way to manage those hunger pangs between lunch and dinner. Instead of reaching for coffee, grab a mug of beef broth! This recipe takes a while to prepare, so you will have to practice patience when making it. Let it cook for a couple of days on your stove, and all those vital minerals in the bones will be soaked up by the broth.

This is a great drink for people who are running low on minerals, especially if you are feeling a bit run down during those cold winter days.

Serves: 4

Ingredients:

16 cups (1 gallon) cold water
3lbs meaty neck bones or ribs
4lbs knuckle bones, marrow, or leftover beef
¼ cup vinegar
3 carrots, coarsely chopped
3 onions, coarsely chopped
Celtic sea salt

Method:

Take all the meaty bones and place them into a large roasting pan. Put the pan in the oven for about an hour, at 350° F. The meat and bones should be well-browned.

While the meaty bones are roasting, take a stock pot, and toss all the bare marrow bones inside. Pour the water, vegetables and vinegar inside. Allow the mixture to sit as the rest of the bones continue roasting.

Take the roasted bones out of the oven, and add them to the stock pot. Pour some hot water into the roasting pan to bring up the small brown pieces stuck in it, and then pour it into the stock pot. Make sure that the bones are totally covered with water.

Heat the water till it boils, then scoop out the foam that floats to the top. Leave the fat floating in the water. Lower the heat, cover and allow it to simmer for between 12 to 72 hours. Longer cooking times bring out the rich flavor of the bones.

If you like to eat marrow, you can salvage some of it from the bones after 3 hours of simmering. Use a pair of tongs to grab the marrow bones and use a small knife to extract the marrow. Then return the bones back into the stockpot.

After 12 to 72 hours, you will have a pot full of brown liquid, with fatty gelatinous globs floating in it. Use a slotted spoon to remove the bones, and then sieve the broth into a big bowl. Pour into mason jars, and allow the broth to cool before refrigerating.

Pork Chop Tonkotsu Broth

This tonkotsu recipe does not need too many bones

to make. It is a basic pork broth that is easy to make and tastes great. The chicken base actually serves to enhance the flavor of the dish.

Serves: 2

Ingredients:

1 bone-in pork chop
2 tsp chicken soup base
¼ onion
1 clove garlic
4 cups water

Method:

Cut the bones and meat into small sections, and then put them in a pan.
Pour the water into the pan, and add onions, garlic, and chicken soup base.
Heat at medium-low, and cover the pan. Allow to simmer for 6 hours, adding water as required.
Sieve the broth into a bowl. Take the pieces of meat and ½ the broth and pour into the blender. After blending, pour the mixture back into the broth in the pan. Mix well.
Serve and enjoy!

Fish Stock

You can use fish stock as a good base for making Asian soups, seafood soups or fish chowder. Fish broth contains extremely high levels of minerals and calcium, not to mention iodine, which is great for thyroid health.

Serves: 4

Ingredients:

2lbs fish bones and heads

4 inch piece of Kombu seaweed

2 onions

1 lemon

2 carrots

1 garlic clove, chopped

3 celery stocks

Thyme

2 bay leaves

Black peppercorns

Method:

Dice up all the vegetables.

Toss the fish bones, vegetable pieces, lemon, spices and kombu into a pot.

Pour in cold water to cover all the ingredients, and simmer for half an hour over medium heat.

Remove scum that forms on the surface, and strain the liquid.

Allow the broth to cool, pour it into a container and refrigerate.

Salmon Chowder

This dish is great for occasions when are feeling under the weather. It is delicious and rich in calcium and iodine, minerals that are important for bones and glandular health. The salmon heads contain the thyroid gland of the fish, so this also adds more nutritional value to boost your thyroid gland.

Serves: 2

Ingredients:

½lb salmon, skinned and chopped into 1-inch chunk

5 cups salmon stock (add more if needed)

Sunflower oil

4 large sweet potatoes, peeled and chopped

1 lemon

1 garlic clove, chopped

1 onion, diced

Sea salt

½ cup yogurt (optional)

2 sprigs thyme, chopped

Method:

Sauté the onions and potatoes in sunflower oil, till the onions are translucent and potatoes partially soft.
Toss in the garlic.
Pour in the stock and simmer.
Throw in the salmon chunks, stir, and cook for an additional 4 minutes till the salmon becomes flaky. Remove from heat.
Pour in the yogurt, and then add the lemon juice and salt.
Pour half the chowder into a blender and blend to make it a bit creamy. The other half should remain chunky.
Pour all the chowder into a bowl, and garnish with parsley or cilantro.

Seafood Gumbo Stock

This is a richly flavored and aromatic seafood stock.

The shrimp shells are simmered slowly to release all the nourishing goodness of omega-3 fatty acids and anti-inflammatory nutrients.

Serves: 8

Ingredients:

1lb shrimp shells

20 cups (1.25 gallons) water

3 cloves garlic, sliced

4 onions, sliced

2 bay leaves

4 carrots, diced

2 sprigs fresh parsley

½ bunch celery, sliced

1 tbsp dried basil

2 tsp dried thyme

1 tsp black pepper, ground

Method:

Place the shrimp shells in an oven set to 375° F. Let them turn brown and dry.

Take a large pot, and pour the water in. Toss in the shrimp shells, onions, thyme, carrots, basil, celery, black pepper, cloves, parsley and garlic. Allow to boil slowly.

Cook for 8 hours on low heat. Add water at various intervals, if necessary.

Strain the stock into a large bowl. Return stock back to the pot, and heat till it reduces to about 12 cups.

Beef and Vegetable Winter Soup

If you are looking for a soup that will provide all the great benefits of bone broth as well as impress your dinner guests during those frigid winter evenings, then this is it! This is a flavorful dish that tingles the taste buds as warms you all over, thanks to the spices and herbs. It is easy to make, and it will be ready in about 1 hour.

Serves: 4

Ingredients:

6 cups beef bone broth
2 pounds boneless beef chuck roast, sliced into 1" chunks
2 sweet potatoes, chopped into cubes
1 rutabaga, chopped into cubes
2 garlic cloves, minced

½ cup onions, finely chopped

2 carrots, chopped

2 cups riced cauliflower

2 parsnips, chopped

1 tbsp parsley, minced

½ tbsp dried thyme

Freshly ground black pepper

Sea salt

Cooking oil

Method:

Place a large saucepan over medium heat, and pour in some cooking oil.

Cook the beef until each side is brown, and then put it aside.

Cook the garlic and onion for about 5 minutes.

Pour ½ of the bone broth into the pan in order to deglaze it.

Toss in the vegetables and cook them for 10 minutes. Stir frequently till the vegetables become soft.

Take the beef, and add it into the saucepan. Pour the remainder of the stock and cover the pan.

Simmer under medium-low heat for ¾ of an hour, till the meat is properly cooked.

Add the fresh parsley, season to taste and serve.

Bone Broth Green Soup

All the veggies in this recipe are good sources of minerals and vitamins, and so is the bone broth. It is a recipe that is perfect for strengthening aching joints and boosting the immune system. It may seem a bit bland but season it well, and it will surprise you!

Serves: 4

Ingredients:

4 cups homemade bone broth
1 head cauliflower
2 tbsp butter
2 cups spinach
1 sweet potato
1 clove garlic, chopped
½ onion, chopped
Sea salt and pepper

Method:

Sauté the onions, butter and garlic in a large pan. Wait till the onions turn clear.
Pour the broth into the pan and stir. Make sure the gelatin melts.

Peel the sweet potato, chop it together with the cauliflower and toss them into the pan.
Boil for a few minutes then reduce to low heat. Make sure the cauliflower and sweet potato become soft. Remove pan from heat. Toss in the spinach, stir, and let spinach wilt (about 5 minutes). Add salt and pepper. Blend the entire mixture till it becomes creamy.

Tom Kha Ghai Soup

This is an authentic Thai dish made from coconut milk and chicken bone broth. The creamy and savory flavor is perfect comfort food when battling sore throats and colds. The broth is full of minerals that aid digestion and electrolytes that make you heal faster. It is a powerhouse of an immune booster!

Serves: 4

Ingredients:

4 cups chicken broth
1 lemon
1.5 cups coconut milk
1 tsp ginger, grated
1 green onion, chopped
¼ tsp dry chili flakes

Sea salt

Cilantro, chopped

Method:

Boil the chicken stock in a pot over medium heat. Remove any scum from the surface.
Add the coconut milk, ginger, chili flakes and lemon juice. Allow to simmer for 20 minutes.
Season with the salt, and then pour into soup bowls. Top off with the green onions and cilantro.

Carrot, Ginger and Coconut Soup

If you're looking for an on-the-go soup, then you will enjoy this creamy, sweet and spicy meal. It offers the perfect balance of healthy fats, gelatin, protein and veggies that you and the whole family will definitely enjoy. Cheers!

Serves: 4

Ingredients:

3 cups chicken bone broth

1lb carrots

2-inch piece of ginger, chopped

3 tbsp olive oil

1 cup coconut milk

1-inch lemon grass, minced (the white part)

1 onion, chopped

Sea salt

Method:

Take a large saucepan and toss in the olive oil, onions, carrots, lemongrass, ginger and salt. Heat for 10 minutes over medium-heat, and stir frequently.

Pour in the broth and the coconut milk. Keep stirring and then raise the temperature to medium-high. Let it simmer before reducing the heat back to a medium level. Allow the soup to simmer for another 15 minutes or till the carrots soften.

Pour the soup into a blender, and blend until the puree achieves a smooth consistency. If the quantity is too much, blend it in two batches.

Season according to taste, and serve!

Keep leftovers refrigerated for 1 week, or freeze for longer use.

Persian Soup

Also known as matzo ball soup, this recipe is a serious

life-saver when battling coughs, colds and tummy aches. The cardamom and turmeric soothe the stomach, and the bone broth boosts the immune system. The result is a protein-packed, flavorful delicacy.

Serves: 4

Ingredients:

12 cups (3/4 gallon) chicken stock
1lb ground turkey
1 egg
2 cups chickpea flour
2 yellow onions
Sea salt
¼ cup fresh lemon juice
1 carrot, sliced
3 garlic cloves, mashed
2 cups parsley
2 tsp ground cardamom
2 cups cooked chickpeas
2 tbsp grape seed oil
1 tsp ground turmeric
Freshly ground black pepper

Method:

Puree the onions into a food processor. In a bowl, whisk together the onions, egg, turmeric, cardamom, black pepper, 2 tsp salt, garlic, and grape seed oil. Add the ground turkey and chickpea flour, and stir. Refrigerate for 4 hours.

After cooling, wet your hands and use them to form small balls of flour.

Take a large pot and boil the broth. Slowly drop the dumplings into the broth and cover. Lower heat and simmer for 50 minutes.

Remove the cooked dumplings. Raise heat and toss in the chickpeas and carrots into the broth. Once the broth is boiling, reduce heat and simmer for 15 minutes. Season with lemon juice, salt and pepper.

Place about 4 matzo balls per serving bowl, and scoop the broth over the top. Season to taste.

Pho Chicken Bone Broth

This bone broth soup from Vietnam contains ingredients that are good for healing the gut as well as providing anti-inflammatory properties. It is perfect for people who are coming down with a cold or the flu, as the peppers provide antiviral and antibacterial protection. The cilantro helps remove heavy metal toxins from the body, while garlic is known to prevent certain cancers and protect your heart.

Serves 4

Ingredients:

1 large free-range organic chicken

4 tbsp fish sauce

1 onion

2 tbsp coconut sugar

1 bag kelp noodles

2 cups bean sprouts

2 garlic cloves, sliced

3-inch ginger piece

2 limes

2 tbsp apple cider vinegar

½ bunch cilantro, chopped

2 tbsp coriander seeds

1 tsp anise seed

4 red organic Fresno chili peppers

1 tsp whole loves

1 bunch basil

Chili sauce

Method:

Place the chicken in a crockpot, submerge it in water, and boil the water for about 5 hours. Use a thermometer to ensure the chicken temperature is 180°F.

Remove the chicken, but keep the water in the crockpot.

On a baking sheet, strip the meat off of the chicken. Store the chicken meat in the refrigerator for later use. Take the chicken carcass and skin and toss it back into the water in the crockpot.

Top off the crockpot with water, and then add garlic and apple cider vinegar.

Cook for 24 hours. In the 23rd hour, toss in the ginger, onions, spices and cilantro stems. Continue cooking.

Sieve the broth into a large bowl, removing the carcass and the spices.

You can store the broth in mason jars and refrigerate for later use, or immediately proceed with the next steps.

Clean out the crockpot, and then pour in the broth, kelp noodles, cilantro leaves, fish sauce, coconut sugar, and chicken meat (from the fridge).

Heat at a low temperature, till it achieves your desired temperature.

Garnish with the bean sprouts, basil leaves, lime wedges, chili sauce, and Fresno chili peppers.
Serve and enjoy!

Pork Ramen Noodle Soup with Roasted Acorn Squash

This recipe is perfectly suited for those freezing days when the sunshine disappears for days. The caramelized pork is simply delectable!

The glucosamine in bone broth can actually stimulate the growth of new collagen, repair damaged joints and reduce pain and inflammation. Additionally, the calcium, magnesium and phosphorus in this bone broth help the bones to grow and repair themselves.

Serves 4

Ingredients:

For the soup

4 cups chicken bone broth
2lbs pork shoulder roast
2 cups mushrooms
¼ cup brown sugar

¼ cup rice vinegar

½ cup soy sauce (low sodium)

4 fried eggs

4 packets ramen noodles

2 tbsp sesame oil

1 tsp black pepper

1 lime

1 tbsp chili paste

1 tbsp ginger

2 tbsp red curry paste

Sliced jalapenos and chopped carrots

For the curry roasted acorn squash

1 tbsp curry powder

1 medium acorn squash, cubed

1 tbsp brown sugar

1 tbsp white miso paste

2 tbsp coconut oil

Pepper to taste

Method:

Place the pork and chicken broth into a crockpot. Pour in the rice vinegar and soy sauce. Throw in the brown sugar, black pepper, lime juice, chili paste, ginger and red curry paste. Cover and cook over low heat for 8 hours.

Preheat oven to 400° F.

Whisk the curry powder, coconut oil, brown sugar, pepper, and miso in a small bowl. Place the squash chunks on a baking sheet, spread the curry mixture over them, and toss thoroughly. Bake 40 minutes, and toss frequently till light brown.

In the meantime, take the pork out of the crockpot and shred it. Add mushrooms to the crockpot and raise heat to high.

Place a large pan over medium heat, pour in the sesame oil, and then add the pork. Pour brown sugar, 2 tablespoons soy sauce and 2 tablespoons rice vinegar over the pork. Wait 2 minutes for the pork to caramelize. Then stir and leave for another 3 minutes. Throw the noodles into the crockpot, cook for 5 minutes and add in half of the pork.

Pour soup into serving bowls and add the roasted acorn squash, the pork, and the fried egg. Garnish with jalapenos and carrots.

Serve and enjoy!

Ginger, Beet and Coconut Soup

Beet soup is a delicious meal that can be consumed cold

or hot, which means we can add a lot of diverse flavors. The ginger gives a tinge of flavor that wonderfully balances the sweetness of the beet. The coconut milk adds healthy fats topped with orange as a garnish. A truly balanced, sumptuous and healthy soup dish!

Serves: 6

Ingredients:

1 thumb-sized ginger piece, chopped

1 cup coconut milk

1 tbsp olive oil

2 lbs beets (remove the greens)

1 small orange, quartered

3 cups chicken bone broth

1 small shallot, chopped

½ cup white wine

3 garlic cloves, minced

3 sprigs fresh rosemary

Zest of 1 orange, finely grated

1 tbsp white wine vinegar

1 tsp sea salt

Method:

Pour the olive oil into a large pot, and heat over medium heat.

Sauté the shallot, garlic, ginger, rosemary and salt for 10 minutes, and stir frequently.

Pour in the white wine, and simmer for 5 minutes. Let the alcohol cook off.

Toss in the bone broth, coconut milk, white wine vinegar and beets. Cover and let simmer for 45 minutes.

Pour some iced water into a bowl. Take the beets out of the pot and place them in the cold water. When the beets become cold to the touch, peel off the skins. Chop up the beets and toss the chunks back into the simmering pot for another 10 minutes.

Pour the mixture into a blender and blend till smooth. Add some of the zest, and serve with the orange pieces as a garnish.

Roasted Tomato, Kale and Sausage Soup

This is an old-school recipe that is still relevant to this day. It is simple to make, and contains a bit of everything for a balanced diet. Kale is low in calorie, high in fiber and has zero fat. One cup of kale has only 36 calories, 5 grams of fiber and 0 grams of fat. It is great for aiding in digestion and elimination with its great fiber content. The sausages and potatoes will leave you with a full feeling, as the broth warms your bones and your soul!

Serves: 6

Ingredients:

1 14-ounce can of roasted tomatoes, diced

4 ounces kales, sliced

20 ounces raw turkey sausage

4 cups chicken bone broth

2 onions, diced

1 cup dry white wine

12 ounces red potatoes, diced

2 cups water

2 tbsp grapeseed oil

1 tsp red pepper flakes, crushed

8 garlic cloves, chopped

4 stalks celery, diced

Freshly ground black pepper

Salt to taste

Method:

Put oil in a crockpot, and heat over medium heat.
Cook the sausages till brown. Remove from pot and put aside.
Reduce heat to medium-low, and sauté the onions. Add salt, pepper, garlic and celery. Let the celery wilt slightly, before pouring in the wine. Stir frequently over a 2 minute period till the alcohol evaporates.
Pour in the broth, water, tomatoes and potatoes. Increase heat and boil well, and then turn down heat. Cover partially and cook for about 15 minutes.
Cut the sausages into ½-inch sections. Toss them and the kale into the pot. Let the kales wilt and the sausages cook through, then season accordingly.
Serve immediately!

Shrimp Gumbo

This seafood dish not only smells and tastes good, but it also provides you with anti-inflammatory protection. Shrimp is a good source of vitamin B12. This vitamin is important for the proper brain function and essential for the formation and maturation of blood cells. Shrimp is also a good source of omega-3 fatty acids which reduce the risk of cardiovascular problems because it reduces cholesterol in the blood.

This New Orleans inspired gumbo is a delicious and healthy treat for those cold winter nights.

Serves 4

Ingredients:

1 pound large shrimp, shells removed

4 cups shrimp stock

1 cup onion, diced

1 cup tomatoes, diced

¼ cup arrowroot powder

½ cup bell pepper, diced

½ cup celery, diced

3 scallions, chopped

½ pound andouille sausage, sliced

1 bay leaf

1/8 tsp freshly ground black pepper

1 tsp fresh thyme, chopped

¼ tsp cayenne pepper

2 garlic cloves, mashed

4 tbsp butter

1 tbsp gumbo file

1 tbsp sea salt

Cauliflower rice (optional)

Method:

Put 1 tablespoon of butter in a large pot, and heat over medium heat. Cook the garlic, onions, bell peppers and celery for 8 minutes. Stir occasionally, and then add in the cayenne, black pepper, tomatoes, thyme, bay leaf, gumbo file and sea salt. Stir continuously while cooking for 5 minutes.

Take a saucepan, place over medium heat, and add 2 tablespoons of butter and ½ cup of shrimp stock. Stir frequently and cook for 5 minutes. Pour in the arrowroot powder, whisking and stirring for 5 minutes. It should form a roux and thicken.

Pour 1 cup of shrimp stock into the saucepan and simmer for 5 minutes. Stir frequently.

Pour another 2 cups of shrimp stock into the pot, raise the heat to medium-high, and add the roux from the saucepan into the pot. Stir well. Bring to a boil and then reduce heat to simmer.

Let it cook for 5 minutes to thicken, turn off heat, and toss in the shrimp.

Add 1 tablespoon of butter to a pan, and sauté the sausage over medium-high heat till each side is browned. Pour in the ½ cup of shrimp stock remaining, and then add the sausage and stock into the large pot. Stir well and get rid of the bay leaf.

Garnish the gumbo with the chopped scallions and spread the gumbo over cauliflower rice. Alternatively, you can eat it as it is.

Chicken and Bacon Orzo Soup

This soup recipe is the perfect comfort food when you need it and is great for keeping warm during those cold winter days. Researchers at the University of Nebraska Medical Center have studied chicken soup's ability to inhibit neutrophil migration and thus mitigate the symptoms of the common cold and other respiratory tract infections.

Indeed, their research indicates that homemade, old-fashioned chicken soup due to its highly anti-inflammatory properties holds significant promise in managing the symptoms of upper respiratory tract infections like colds. Plus, it's easy to make – you'll be done in under an hour!

Serves: 6

Ingredients:

6 cups chicken bone broth
1lb boneless chicken breast
5 slices bacon

1 cup carrots, chopped

½ cup orzo

1 cup celery, chopped

2 cloves garlic, mashed

2 cups onions, chopped

Fresh parsley, chopped

½ tsp freshly ground black pepper

½ tsp salt

Method:

Using a pan with a heavy bottom, render the fat from the bacon over low heat. When the fat forms a layer at the bottom, increase the heat slightly and cook the bacon.

Line a plate with paper towels and transfer the bacon to the plate.

Remove all but 2 tablespoons of fat from the pan. Toss in the onions, carrots, celery and garlic into the pan. Add the salt and cook over medium heat for 5 minutes. Stir until they caramelize.

Place the chicken pieces on the veggies and pour in the broth. Once the liquid starts to boil, cover and turn down heat. Let the soup simmer 20 minutes before removing the chicken and shredding it.

As the soup continues to boil, add the orzo. Do not cover. Let the orzo become al dente.

Put the shredded chicken into the soup and add salt and pepper.

Chop up the cooked bacon and parsley, and use as garnish.

Serve.

Mexican Chicken Stew

This dish is easy to make and the array of vegetables makes it a healthy choice indeed. It's great for clearing out stuffy noses and warming you up when you need some comfort food in winter. The black bean's fiber, potassium, folate, vitamin B6 and phytonutrient content, coupled with its lack of cholesterol, all support heart health.

The fiber in black beans helps lower the total amount of cholesterol in the blood and decrease the risk of heart disease. The Mexican spices give it a flavor that will set your taste buds alight.

Serves: 6

Ingredients:

1lb cooked shredded chicken breast
4 cups chicken bone broth
15 ounces black beans

Bone Broth

2 cups water

15 ounces fire roasted tomatoes, diced

1 can corn kernels

3 cloves garlic, mashed

1 tsp garlic powder

1 onion, chopped

1 jalapeno, chopped

½ tsp ground black pepper

2 tsp chili powder

2 tsp ground cumin

1 tsp hot salsa

Salt to taste

1 tsp oregano

1 bell pepper, sliced

Method:

Heat some olive oil in a pot over medium heat. Toss in the onions, jalapenos, garlic and bell peppers. Cook till tender.

Pour in the water, bone broth, red pepper and tomatoes. Cook till the vegetables become soft.

Throw in the black beans, corn, cooked chicken, cumin, garlic powder, chili powder and oregano. Spice it up with the salsa and salt.

Cover and simmer for half an hour. Stir frequently. Serve with baked tortilla.

CHAPTER 5

Bone Broth Drinks and Smoothies

Bone Broth Energy Drink

Always tempted to reach for a hot cup of coffee in the morning? How about a delicious mug of bone broth energy drink instead? It will give you a powerful blast of nutrients to get you through those midmorning energy slumps.

Collard greens are a very good source of vitamins B2, B6, and choline, and a good source of vitamins B1, B3, folate, and pantothenic acid. A well-balanced intake of B vitamins - especially vitamins B6, B12, folate, and choline - can be important in controlling cardiovascular disease risk.

The health benefits of arugula include low risk of cancer, healthy bones and improved eyesight. It has antioxidant properties and is good for maintaining healthy skin.

The veggies and fruits in this drink provide the powerful antioxidants to keep you going for hours!

Serves: 4

Ingredients:

3 cups of bone broth base, unseasoned
4 cups of raw greens (collard greens, arugula, watercress or kale)
4 carrots, coarsely sliced
2 cups of diced sweet fruit (strawberries, oranges, or pineapples)

Method:

Toss all the vegetables and fruits into a high-powered blender, and then pour the bone broth on top.
Blend the mixture till the plants turn to liquid.
If you want to refresh yourself with a cold drink, freeze the fresh fruits and vegetables beforehand. If you crave a warm drink during winter, simply warm the blended

drink over low heat. Avoid simmering or boiling it as you will likely destroy the antioxidant properties in the drink.

Banana Bone Broth Smoothie

This is a tasty, healthy and gelatinous drink. This smoothie is packed with minerals that heal your digestive tract and alleviate joint pain, as well as maintaining the natural flexibility of connective tissue.

Bananas are a very good source of vitamin B6 and a good source of manganese, vitamin C, potassium, dietary fiber, potassium, biotin, and copper. The taste of banana will really come through in this drink, and the taste of the bone broth will be masked to produce a flavorful banana smoothie.

Serves: 2

Ingredients:

2 cups bone broth
1 cup almond milk
½ cup cold water
2 fresh bananas
1 cup blueberries

2 tsp vanilla powder

½ cup coconut shreds

1 tsp honey

Method:

Put all your ingredients in a blender, and blend at high speed for about 1 minute.
Enjoy!

Bone Broth Electrolyte Smoothie

This is a homemade smoothie that will help maintain your fluid levels. It improves your digestion and boosts functioning of your adrenal glands. The sea salt, lemon juice and bone broth provide calcium and improve gut health. The spirulina is a superfood that is packed with essential amino acids, while the blueberries are full of antioxidants.

The blueberry's fiber, potassium, folate, vitamin C, vitamin B6 and phytonutrient content, coupled with its lack of cholesterol, all support heart health. The fiber in blueberries helps lower the total amount of cholesterol in the blood and decrease the risk of heart disease.

Serves: 4

Ingredients:

2 cups bone broth

3 cups blueberries

1 tsp spirulina

½ cup lemon juice

1 tsp vanilla extract

Method:

Using a high-powered blender, blend all the ingredients together for 1 minute, till the berries form a smooth puree.

Serve!

Bone Broth Greens Smoothie

This can be a great breakfast drink or a sumptuous snack. It contains a combination of minerals, proteins, collagen, and vitamins that are good for your bones and digestive health.

Low in fat and even lower in cholesterol, spinach is high in niacin and zinc, as well as protein, fiber, vitamins A, C, E and K, thiamin, vitamin B6, folate, calcium, iron, magnesium, phosphorus, potassium, copper, and manganese.

Coconuts are highly nutritious and rich in fiber, vitamins C, E, B1, B3, B5 and B6 and minerals including iron, selenium, sodium, calcium, magnesium and phosphorous. Unlike cow's milk, coconut milk is lactose free so can be used as a milk substitute by those with lactose intolerance.

The avocado and collagen from the broth end up producing a creamy radiant texture that you will absolutely love!

Serves: 4

Ingredients:

1 can coconut milk
4 cups beef bone broth
1 tbsp apple cider vinegar
½ avocado
3 handfuls kale or spinach
1 cup of mixed berries

Method:

Pour the bone broth and the coconut milk into a blender. Top up with the rest of the ingredients.
Blend for 1 minute.

Serve and enjoy!

Cherry Ghee Smoothie

This smoothie will keep you full for the better part of the day. It contains gelatin which heals the gut, joints, skin as well as curing insomnia. The coconut oil will give you a lot of energy and is actually great for a fat burning metabolism.

Ghee is known to have anti-inflammatory and healing properties. It is rich in conjugated linoleic acid, or CLA, a fatty acid known to be protective against carcinogens, artery plaque and diabetes. Because of these benefits, researchers say ghee can potentially be used to help prevent cardiovascular diseases.

Serves: 2

Ingredients:

½ cup organic cherries

2 cups coconut water

1 tbsp coconut oil

3 large eggs

2 cups chicken broth

1 tbsp nut butter

2 tbsp raw cocoa powder

2 tbsp ghee (clarified butter)

Method:

Pour the coconut water and the chicken broth into a high-power blender. Add the other ingredients.
Blend until a smooth consistency is reached. Drink immediately.
Enjoy!

Carrot and Orange Smoothie

Here comes a smoothie that incorporates the gut-cleansing and healing properties of bone broth, and the infection-fighting properties of vitamins A and C both found in oranges and carrots.

Most of the benefits of carrots can be attributed to their beta carotene and fiber content. This root vegetable is also a good source of antioxidant agents. Furthermore, carrots are rich in vitamin A, Vitamin C, Vitamin K, vitamin B8, pantothenic acid, folate, potassium, iron, copper, and manganese.

Additionally, this smoothie is easy to make and takes very little time to prepare. Oh, and it's wickedly delicious too!

Serves: 2

Ingredients:

2 cups beef bone broth

1 cup carrot juice

Juice from 1 lemon

1 cup fresh orange juice

½ cup ice

¾ tsp ground turmeric

¼ cup fresh pineapple juice

Method:

Pour all the ingredients into a high-powered blender. Blend for approx. 5 minutes, till the consistency is smooth.

Serve and enjoy!

Lime and Coconut Sipping Broth

Adding coconut milk to your bone broth smoothie is a really good way of ensuring that your diet gets a dose of healthy fat. Ginger has a long history of use for relieving digestive problems such as nausea, loss of appetite, motion sickness and pain.

It's a rich source of antioxidants including gingerols, shogaols, zingerones, and more. Ginger actually has broad-spectrum antibacterial, antiviral, antioxidant, and anti-parasitic properties, to name just several of its more than 40 pharmacological actions

This is a flavorful drink that is easy to prepare and will leave you craving some more!

Serves 2

Ingredients:

Juice of 2 limes
1 cup coconut milk
2 cups chicken bone broth
1 tsp sea salt
¼ cup ginger, peeled and minced

Method:

Put all the ingredients into a saucepan and simmer over medium-heat. Cook for 5 minutes.
Pour the mixture into a blender and mix until a smooth consistency is achieved.
Sieve the broth, and then refrigerate.
Serve after smoothie is chilled.

CHAPTER 6

Bone Broth Breakfast Recipes

Bone Broth Latte

How about we turn an ordinary mug of bone broth into a refreshing, delicious, frothy and creamy breakfast drink, fully loaded with healthy protein, fats and minerals?

Adding the collagen peptides help to make it a more complete breakfast, as they are a natural source of healthy proteins. Collagen ensures regeneration and elasticity of joints, hair and skin. Adding the coconut oil and butter give you healthy fats and won't stress your adrenals like caffeine does. A simple and nutritious breakfast meal!

Serves: 2

Ingredients:

2 mugs of chicken bone broth

2 tbsp butter

2 tbsp organic coconut oil

3 scoops collagen

Method:

Bring the bone broth to a boil.
Pour the broth, butter, coconut oil and collagen powder into a high-powered blender. Blend for 20 seconds.
Serve and enjoy!

Curried Scramble with Artichokes

Bone broth may be a powerful and healthy beverage, but the best thing about it is that it can be incorporated into any dish or recipe. In this recipe, curry provides the heat and anti-inflammatory properties to get you ready for a long day, while the tomatoes and artichokes give the dish an element of sumptuous depth.

Curry powder has a number of valuable health benefits, including the prevention of cancer, protection against heart disease, reduction of Alzheimer's disease symptoms, easing pain and inflammation and boosting bone health.

Serves: 2

Ingredients:

4 eggs

½ cup artichoke hearts, quartered

¼ cup bone broth

1 ½ tsp curry powder

1 ½ tsp olive oil

1 tbsp sun-dried tomatoes, chopped

1 sweet potato, diced

Freshly ground black pepper

Sea salt

1 tbsp fresh cilantro, chopped

1 ½ tsp ghee (clarified butter)

Method:

Pour the olive oil into a skillet, and heat over medium heat. Toss in the sweet potato and sauté until tender. Toss in the tomatoes and artichokes, and then stir for 2 more minutes.

Pour in the bone broth and raise the heat to medium-high. Keep stirring as you cook for about 4 minutes, till the broth is totally reduced. Put the mixture on a plate and clean the skillet.

Break the eggs into a bowl, add the curry powder and whisk together. Melt the ghee in the skillet, pour in the egg mixture, and scramble the eggs to your liking. Place the sweet potato mixture and the eggs in one bowl, and then place on two serving plates. Add the cilantro, black pepper and salt to taste.

Not So Basic Eggs in Broth

If you love having a hearty breakfast, and plain broth seems a bit too light, then add some eggs to your broth. Eggs work with almost every type of broth you can think of. Eggs are a very good source of inexpensive, high quality protein. More than half the protein of an egg is found in the egg white along with vitamin B2 and lower amounts of fat and cholesterol than the yolk. The whites are rich sources of selenium, vitamin D, B6, B12 and minerals such as zinc, iron and copper.

This meal provides a good amount of protein that will definitely keep the hunger at bay and help you start your day off right.

Serves: 2

Ingredients:

2 eggs
2 cups of bone broth
3 sprigs chopped parsley
Parmesan cheese, grated
Salt and pepper to taste

Method:

Heat the broth.
Poach the eggs in the simmering broth till the whites cook, but keep the yolks runny.
Top off with the rest of the ingredients.

Asian-style Eggs in Broth

This breakfast dish is similar to the one above, but contains ingredients that add some flavor and zest. The garlic and ginger are classic Asian condiments that are great for boosting your immunity, while the kale is a good source of iron and fiber.

A study published in the *Journal of National Cancer Institute* showed that less than one clove a day may cut prostate-cancer risk in half, and other research links garlic to a lowered incidence of stomach, colon and possibly breast cancers.

Serves: 2

Ingredients:

2 eggs
2 cups bone broth
Chopped kale
2 garlic cloves, chopped
Fish sauce or soy sauce, for seasoning
1-inch ginger piece, chopped

Method:

Heat broth till it simmers. Toss in the garlic and ginger, and allow it to continue simmering for 5 minutes.
Add the kale and eggs. Simmer till the eggs cook and the kale wilts completely.
Use the sauces to season.

Eggs and Sausage in Tomato Basil Broth

This is a sumptuous way to start off your morning.

Plenty of protein to go with your broth which leaves you feeling satiated. The basil leaves add flavor to the meal.

The many health benefits of tomatoes can be attributed to their wealth of nutrients and vitamins, including an impressive amount of vitamins A, C, and K, as well as significant amounts of vitamin B6, folate, and thiamin. Tomatoes are also a good source of potassium, manganese, magnesium, phosphorous, and copper.

Tomatoes help to build strong bones. The vitamin K and calcium in tomatoes are both very good for strengthening and repairing bones.

Lycopene also has been shown to improve bone mass, which is a great way to fight osteoporosis.

Serves: 2

Ingredients:

2 eggs
2 cups beef or chicken bone broth
½ link sausage, chopped and sautéed
4 basil leaves, chopped
1 tsp tomato paste
Salt and pepper

Methods:

Heat the broth till it simmers. Pour out ½ cup into a bowl, add the tomato paste, and pour back into the broth. Mix thoroughly.
Add the eggs and poach for 3 minutes, and then add the sausages.
Add the basil with salt and pepper to taste.

Savory Oatmeal with Fried Egg and Sriracha

Oatmeal and bone broth may not seem compatible but this combination is dynamite! The whey and lemon juice help make the oats more digestible and cook faster.

Oatmeal contains both calcium and potassium which are known to reduce blood pressure numbers. Eating oats is linked to an average 7% drop in LDL cholesterol, research shows. Many other things also affect your heart's health (like what else you eat, how active you are, and whether you smoke), but oatmeal is a simple heart-smart start.

This is a hearty and balanced meal that gives you all the energy you need to start your day.

Serves: 2

Ingredients:

1 cup oatmeal

2 cups water

2 eggs, fried

2 cups beef or chicken bone broth

Sriracha to taste

2 tsp whey

½ cup lemon juice

2 garlic cloves, chopped

Soy or Worcestershire sauce

Method:

Warm the water and soak the oatmeal in it. Add the whey and lemon juice, and soak overnight.

Drain the water from the oatmeal. Pour the oatmeal and bone broth into a bowl, add the garlic, and simmer for 5 minutes.

Season with soy or Worcestershire sauce and top off with the sriracha and fried eggs.

Baked Sweet Potato Spiced Donut

How about a bone broth dish that is healthy and

satisfies your sweet tooth as well? This delicious snack offers you a great way to start your day, and can also serve as a midmorning treat.

Sweet potatoes pack a powerful nutritional punch. They have got over 400% of your daily needs for vitamin A in one medium spud, as well as loads of fiber and potassium. Many studies have suggested that increasing consumption of plant foods like sweet potatoes decreases the risk of obesity, diabetes, heart disease and overall mortality while promoting a healthy complexion, increased energy, and overall lower weight.

Serves: 4

Ingredients

½ cup bone broth, strained

½ cup sweet potatoes (skinned, cooked and mashed)

½ cup coconut flour

¾ cup almond flour

5 eggs, large

½ cup pure maple syrup

1 tsp baking soda

¼ cup coconut oil

½ tsp nutmeg, finely ground

1 tsp vanilla extract

1 tsp ground cinnamon

1 tsp ground ginger

¼ tsp sea salt

¼ tsp ground cloves

¼ tsp ground cardamom

Chocolate-Bacon Glazing:

2 pieces of crisp bacon, cooled, dried and crumbled

¼ cup dark chocolate, chopped and melted

1 tsp honey

1 ½ tsp melted coconut oil

Method:

Preheat the oven to 350° F, and coat the interior of the baking pan with oil.

Put the sweet potato, eggs, maple syrup, vanilla, coconut oil and bone broth into a blender. Mix for 15 seconds until the mixture turns frothy.

Add the rest of the dry ingredients to the blended mix. Blend slowly for 10 seconds and then blend on high power for another 20 seconds.

Fill 2/3 of the baking pan with the mixture.

Put the pan in the oven for 20 minutes. Allow the donuts to cool in the pan for 10 minutes, before removing and placing them on a cooling rack.

The Glazing:

Place the chocolate, coconut oil and honey into a shallow bowl and whisk together to achieve a smooth consistency.
Holding a donut upside down, dip the top part of every donut into the chocolate mix. Allow the excess glaze to drip off by rotating the donut gently. Flip the donut upright and return it to the rack.
Sprinkle the bacon crumbs onto the glazed donut. Do this before the chocolate glaze gets hard.
Leave the donuts for about 5 minutes, before refrigerating for 15 minutes so that the glaze hardens.

Bone Broth Lemon Glazed Dessert Loaf

This broth-based recipe is great for preparing over the weekend so that you have something healthy and nutritious to eat during your week.

Yields 1 loaf of bread, approximately 16-18 slices

Ingredients:

¾ cup beef bone broth, strained and fat removed

2/3 cup coconut flour

6 eggs

1 tsp baking soda

¼ tsp sea salt

Lemon zest

¼ cup melted coconut oil

1/3 cup honey

¼ cup lemon juice

Lemon Glaze:

Juice from one lemon and zest

2 tbsp raw honey

½ tsp vanilla extract

2 tbsp ghee (clarified butter), melted

2 tbsp coconut milk, full fat

Method:

Preheat oven to 350° F.
Mix the bread ingredients together into a bowl.
Grease the baking pan well before pouring the dough into it. Bake till golden brown.

Allow cooling for ten minutes before removing from pan, and then cool it on a rack completely.

Glazing Method:

Combine all glaze ingredients and heat in a small pot till it begins to simmer.
Remove from heat and allow to cool. Then refrigerate to firm it up.
Drizzle the glaze on top of the cooled loaf.
Place the loaf in a fridge for an hour to make the glaze firmer. The glaze shouldn't become hard.
Place the loaf in a plastic container, cover and store in the fridge.

Gluten Free Stuffing with Sausage

This is an innovative recipe for those who want to stay gluten free and still enjoy a sumptuous breakfast with bone broth. The bread, cauliflower and sausages may play a major role in this dish, but the bone broth gives it all the nutritious minerals and amino acids that your gut needs to stay healthy. This is a versatile recipe, so feel free to add or remove any minor ingredient depending on your food intolerances.

Serves: 4

Ingredients:

1 gluten-free loaf of bread (e.g. coconut bread), chopped into ¾-inch cubes

1 cup bone broth

1 head cauliflower, chopped

1 pound sausages

2 onions, chopped

½ cup melted butter

8 celery stalks, thinly sliced

1 tsp sea salt

2 tsp dried sage

2 tsp dried thyme

Method:

Preheat the oven to 375° F.

Heat 2 tablespoons of butter in a large skillet, and then sauté the cauliflower over medium-low heat. Add 1 teaspoon of salt and stir frequently for twenty minutes. Remove the cauliflower and place it in a large bowl. Add 2 more tablespoons of butter to the skillet and sauté the celery and onions over medium-low heat. Add 1 teaspoon of salt and cook for twenty minutes.

Pour water into a saucepan, add salt, and let the sausages simmer for 12 minutes. Once ready, let the sausages cool.

Cut them into small bits and toss them into the bowl of sautéed cauliflower.

Throw the sautéed celery and onions to the bowl.

Add the bone broth, melted butter, bread pieces, pepper, salt, and spices into the bowl.

Grease a large casserole dish. Fold the ingredients together lightly, and then place the stuffing into the casserole dish.

Bake until the top turns golden brown.

Bone Broth with Sausage and Greens

This is a simple and creative recipe that you can switch up any way you like. This dish is packed with super-nutrients and bone-strengthening minerals, such as calcium and phosphorous. It has vital proteins and vitamins to help you keep away those pesky colds and flu.

Dulse is a red seaweed harvested in the cool waters along Atlantic coast of Canada. Red or purple in color, dulse is considered a superfood because of its high iodine and potassium content, plus a long list of micro-nutrients and phytochemicals. Dulse extract has been clinically proven to possess free radical scavenging activity, making dulse useful as an antioxidant. The seaweed has also been demonstrated to inhibit the growth of lipid (fat) cells in the laboratory.

Serves: 1

Ingredients:

Raw pork sausage

2 cups of beef bone broth

1 egg

1 tsp sea salt to taste

1 tsp dulse powder seasoning

2 stalks celery, chopped

4 green peppers, chopped

A handful of chopped cabbage

Method:

Pour the bone broth into a pan, and add some pork sausage. Use the quantity that feels right for you.
Heat the pan over medium heat.
Toss in the chopped celery, peppers and cabbage.
Crack the egg into the pan, and then add the dulse powder and salt. Cook until the sausage is golden brown.
Serve and enjoy!

CHAPTER 7

Bone Broth Sauces and Sides

Bone Broth Tomato Sauce

If you never thought bone broth could be turned to sauce, think again. This tomato sauce recipe is easy to make and very nutritious. What you get is classic tomato sauce for topping noodles, lasagna or pasta.

Serves: 4

Ingredients:

2 cans tomato paste, 6 ounces each
2 cups bone broth
½ tsp dry oregano

1 tbsp freshly ground black pepper

2 tbsp extra virgin oil

½ tsp basil

2 garlic cloves, minced

½ tsp sea salt

Method:

Toss all the ingredients into a medium saucepan. Whisk well.

Place saucepan over medium heat for about 5 minutes. Stir frequently to prevent sputtering.

Lower the heat, cover and let simmer for 5 more minutes. This allows the aroma of dried herbs to come forth and softens the taste of raw garlic.

Turn off heat, but don't uncover the pan.

Prepare your main dish (noodles or pasta).

Serve.

Braised Collard Greens with Bacon

This delicious side dish is easy to make and only takes about half an hour to prepare. The broth, of course, provides the nourishing goodness that will maintain a healthy gut and immune system. Collard greens are a good source of iron and other vital minerals.

Serves: 4

Ingredients:

½ cup bone broth
1 bunch collard greens
4 slices bacon, chopped
Salt

Method:

Put the bacon slices in a pan and cook over medium heat until they become crispy.
Add the greens, and stir well.
Pour in the bone broth, let it simmer, and then lower the heat to medium low.
Stir regularly and continue cooking until the bone broth evaporates and the collard greens wilt. This should take about 20 minutes.

Mashed Yuca with Bone Broth

This is a great Paleo side dish that utilizes the yucca root, an excellent substitute for potatoes. The starchy root of the yucca is not only rich in carbohydrates but also contains a healthy mix of vitamins, minerals and plant-based nutrients.

There is strong evidence that yucca's active components, including steroidal saponins, resveratrol and yuccaols, all seem to exert anti-inflammatory effects that may explain their historic use by folk medicine practitioners to treat arthritis and other inflammatory conditions.

Serves: 2

Ingredients:

1 pound of yuca, coarsely chopped
1 cup chicken broth
4 tbsp olive oil
Black pepper and salt

Method:

Rinse the yuca roots thoroughly under running water. Peel the yuca using a sharp knife, making sure to cut out any parts that appear discolored.
Cut the yuca into 2-inch chunks, and toss them into a pot of water.
Once the water comes to a boil, cover the pot with a lid. Reduce heat and let it simmer.
Cook until the yuca becomes tender and can be pierced with a knife. This takes about 25 minutes.

Remove the tough, stringy part from the center of each yuca piece.

Strain and place the yuca pieces into a large bowl.

Use a potato masher to mash, and then pour in the bone broth and olive oil. Keep mashing until you get a consistency that suits you.

Serve and enjoy!

Bacon and Bone Broth Barbeque Sauce

If you love both barbequing and bacon, and have been searching for a perfect recipe that combines BBQ sauce and bacon, then this is it! This sauce can be used as a dipping sauce or to glaze meat on the grill. The bone broth is tossed in to provide an amazing healing elixir for your gut.

Yields: 2 cups

Ingredients:

1½ cups bone broth
1 tbsp bacon drippings
Juice of 1 lemon
3 garlic cloves, chopped

4 ounce can of tomato paste

¼ cup yellow onion, chopped

½ tsp sea salt

1½ tbsp Dijon mustard

1/8 tsp cayenne pepper

1 tsp apple cider vinegar

2 tsp smoked paprika

1 tsp coconut aminos

Method:

Take a sauce pan and cook the bacon drippings over medium heat.

Toss in the onions and garlic, and sauté.

Add the coconut aminos, mustard, paprika, apple cider vinegar, salt, and cayenne pepper. Sauté for 1 more minute.

Pour in the bone broth, lemon juice and tomato paste. Stir until a smooth consistency is achieved.

Bring to a light boil, then reduce heat and let simmer for 45 minutes.

Store the sauce in a container, and place in the fridge.

Pork Roast Spaghetti Sauce

This is a great recipe that makes use of left over roast

pork bones. The pork bones are used to make delicious bone broth that you can add to your spaghetti sauce for extra nutrients and minerals. The recipe produces about 14 cups of sauce, which is enough for four lbs of spaghetti.

Yields: 28 servings

Ingredients:

2 cups pork bone broth

1 cup red wine

4 cups water

½ tsp dried oregano

3 cloves garlic, crushed

1/8 tsp ground nutmeg

½ tsp dried basil

1 cup mushrooms, sliced

1 tsp Italian-style seasoning

½ cup black olives, sliced

½ tsp dried parsley

1 tsp salt

½ tsp red pepper flakes, crushed

2 tsp sugar

2 bay leaves

1 onion, chopped

1 tsp black pepper, ground

1 tsp celery salt

½ tsp dried rosemary, crushed

3 cups of tomato paste

Method:

Take a pot and put in the garlic, bay leaves, sugar, oregano, nutmeg, onions, celery salt, red pepper, basil, rosemary, water, mushrooms, wine, black pepper, Italian seasoning, parsley, nutmeg, olives, bone broth and tomato paste. Whisk all the ingredients together. Heat the mixture over medium heat for 5 minutes.

Cover the pot, reduce heat and simmer for 2 hours. Stir regularly.

Remove the cover and cook until a thick consistency is achieved.

Serve.

Conclusion

Bone broth may be a nutritious source of health and wellness - that's a fact that cannot be denied. However, bone broth is actually more than that. It's a lifestyle choice. Your aim may be to cure one or two ailments that are bothering you, but by introducing bone broth into your diet, you attain lifelong benefits.

Consuming bone broth should be seen as a way of embracing a holistic, sustainable way of life. The healing attributes of bone broth are phenomenal, to say the least, and if you are serious about healing and wellness, then you are well on your way.

Society today is full of people who are suffering from all kinds of ailments and diseases, some of them incurable. What you put into your mouth is actually the genesis of all your problems. It is also the source of everything that my heal you. That's a powerful fact of life that can be used to your advantage in achieving optimal health.

Years of consuming artificial chemicals and processed junk food may be the reason your gut no longer has the necessary elements to function well. A simple change in diet may be the solution you've been seeking all this time.

The recipes provided in this book are a great place to start your bone broth lifestyle. Bone broth is gut-friendly, gut-healing and gut-soothing. As you try these awesome bone broth recipes out one-by-one, remember to enjoy the experience and have fun being creative in the kitchen. Start today and choose to adopt a diet of real food like our ancestors enjoyed.

If you enjoyed this book, please leave a review on Amazon. Thank you!

Be sure to check out our website at www.thetotalevolution.com for more information.

Thank you!

Preview Of 'Mediterranean Diet: The Complete Mediterranean Diet For Beginners With 101 Heart Healthy Recipes'

The Mediterranean Diet has evolved naturally and is the result of many centuries of cross-cultural exchange and refinement.

It is not a diet in the strictest sense but rather a natural dietary tradition. It is therefore easier to adapt to because it is wholesome in its approach and contains comparatively fewer restrictions than most other modern diet plans.

Go on a journey to the center of culinary history.

The Mediterranean Diet is among one of the oldest diets known to man. It comes from a region where some of the earliest civilizations in the western world originated, the Greek and the Roman civilizations.

The meaning of the term 'Mediterranean' which comes from Latin can be interpreted as "in between lands" or "in the middle of the earth." This is significant since the Mediterranean Sea is situated where three continents –Africa, Asia and Europe – meet.

Just as the Mediterranean region represents a geographical and cultural crossroad, the Mediterranean Diet is a combination of different culinary traditions. It is important to understand that the Mediterranean Diet represents not just a way of eating but a way of life.

It makes sense therefore to adapt the Mediterranean Diet in a holistic manner by more than just choosing the right kind of food but also by preparing and eating it the way the ancient Greeks and the Romans did.

Needless to say, combining the Mediterranean Diet with an active lifestyle will make it more enjoyable and produce healthier results.

How did the Mediterranean Diet gain popularity?

Awareness about the Mediterranean Diet in America and the rest of the world can be traced to studies conducted in the 1960s by Dr Ancel Keys, an American scientist who was interested in the relationship between diet and health in general and between diet and disease prevention in particular.

He studied the dietary habits of the inhabitants of different countries in order to determine why Americans despite having what was then believed to be a healthy diet were more susceptible to heart diseases than some Europeans.

The findings clearly indicated that the American diet was more similar to the eating habits of the inhabitants of many north European countries. The dietary traditions of these countries predominantly consisted of meat, butter, dairy and animal fats and a comparatively lesser amount of fish, fruits and vegetables.

In sharp contrast, the inhabitants of the Mediterranean region, especially Greece and Italy, including the islands of Crete and Sardinia, consumed fresh fish, fruits and vegetables on a daily basis while eating meat, eggs and dairy products in moderation.

What are the benefits of the Mediterranean Diet?

The Greek and the Italians had remarkable longevity while enjoying great health, and most of them were living completely disease-free lives. Most significant was the near absence of common modern day diseases like asthma, diabetes and cancer, as well as very low incidence of cardiovascular disease and chronic obstructive pulmonary disease.

Dr. Keys' theory was that the people who lived around the region bordering the Mediterranean Sea were healthier mainly because of their diet.

More recent studies have indicated that this diet along with the active yet relaxed and stress-free lifestyle of the area's inhabitants, contributed to improving metabolism, controlling cholesterol and blood sugar levels and preventing the onset of most modern ailments like diabetes and heart disease.

The evidence for the truism, we are what we eat, has never been more pronounced than in the case of the Mediterranean Diet. While there are many studies that establish the healthy attributes of eating like the people in the Mediterranean region, a simpler way to approach things is to just look at the delicious variety of dishes that constitute the Mediterranean Diet.

Lose weight without losing heart.

From bruschetta to paella, from the gazpacho to the anytime snack of falafel, from the irresistible baba ghanoush to the tantalizing tzatziki, the Mediterranean Diet is as much an epicurean delight as it is a healthy diet. It is perhaps the only diet where eating is not associated with guilt or restriction but with pleasure.

If you want to get healthy and lose excess weight, wouldn't you like to enjoy it? Instead of asking you to give up eating food that you enjoy or asking you to eat less, the Mediterranean Diet recommends that you eat abundantly, albeit the right kind of food.

The Mediterranean Diet is the perfect way of eating to follow if you want to lose weight and keep it off for life!

Mediterranean Diet: The Complete Mediterranean Diet For Beginners With 101 Heart Healthy Recipes is available for purchase on Amazon.com.

Our Other Books

Below you'll find some of our other books that are popular on Amazon.com and the international sites.

Mayo Clinic Diet: A Proven Diet Plan For Lifelong Weight Loss

Master Cleanse: How To Do A Natural Detox The Right Way And Lose Weight Fast

The Dukan Diet: A High Protein Diet Plan To Lose Weight And Keep It Off For Life

Glycemic Index Diet: A Proven Diet Plan For Weight Loss and Healthy Eating With No Calorie Counting

Clean Eating Diet: A 10 Day Diet Plan To Eat Clean, Lose Weight And Supercharge Your Body

Wheat Belly: The Anti-Diet - A Guide To Gluten Free Eating And A Slimmer Belly

IIFYM: Flexible Dieting - Sculpt The Perfect Body

While Eating The Foods You Love

Mediterranean Diet: 101 Ultimate Mediterranean Diet Recipes To Fast Track Your Weight Loss & Help Prevent Disease

Acid Reflux Diet: A Beginner's Guide To Natural Cures And Recipes For Acid Reflux, GERD And Heartburn

Hypothyroidism Diet: Natural Remedies & Foods To Boost Your Energy & Jump Start Your Weight Loss

It Starts With Food: A 30 Day Diet Plan To Reset Your Body, Lose Weight And Become A Healthier You

Printed in Great Britain
by Amazon